WALT WHITMAN

I Hear America Singing

illustrated by ROBERT SABUDA

PHILOMEL BOOKS / NEW YORK

For my grandmother Nina

— R. S.

Illustration copyright © 1991 by Robert Sabuda
Introduction copyright © 1991 by Lisa Tracy
Philomel Books, a division of The Putnam & Grosset Book Group,
200 Madison Avenue, New York, NY 10016.
Published simultaneously in Canada.
Printed in Hong Kong by South China Printing Co. (1988) Ltd.
Book design by Gunta Alexander
The text was set in Meridien
Library of Congress Cataloging-in-Publication Data
Whitman, Walt, 1819-1892.
I hear America singing / by Walt Whitman.
p. cm. Summary: Whitman's famous poem, here illustrated,
depicts people at work all over nineteenth-century America.
ISBN 0-399-21808-4
1. Children's poetry, American. [1. Occupations—Poetry. 2. American poetry.]
I. Title. PS3222.I18 1991 811'.3—dc20 90-19709 CIP AC
10 9 8 7 6 5 4 3 2 1
First impression

INTRODUCTION

Walter Whitman, considered by many to be America's greatest poet, loved America and all he saw in it, especially its people. Whitman, who preferred to be known as Walt, was born May 31, 1819, the second child of Walter Whitman and Louisa Van Velsor Whitman. His father was a housebuilder in the farmlands of Long Island, outside of New York City. When Walt was four years old, the family moved to Brooklyn, New York.

Both his father and his mother came from families that had settled on Long Island before the American Revolution. Growing up, he and his family—including seven brothers and sisters—traveled back and forth from Brooklyn to the seashore of Long Island.

Whitman attended school only until he was eleven years old. He then went to work—which was not unusual for children at that time—first as an office boy for a lawyer. He soon became interested in printing and journalism, and he worked in both professions as a young man. He also learned carpentry from his father and worked in the family business building houses to earn extra money. For a short time, he worked as a teacher.

All the while, he was writing. His writings eventually grew into a group of poems that he published in 1855 called *Leaves of Grass*. Whitman kept adding poems to *Leaves of Grass* whenever he had new experiences, and he made it very clear right from the beginning that he was going to write about all Americans: rich, poor, men, women, workers, children, all races and ethnic groups. He was going to write about the individual. His first words in his book were, ''I celebrate myself,'' and he followed that by declaring, ''For every atom belonging to me as good belongs to you.''

In his life, Whitman experienced the horror of the Civil War, the death of Abraham Lincoln, the pleasure of working with his hands, and the fascination of just watching people. He wrote about all these experiences in his poetry.

One of Whitman's most famous poems, ''I Hear America Singing'' is a good way to get to know Whitman and his poetry, which does not rhyme. This style was largely invented by Whitman.

This book introduces Whitman and his America. After reading it, to know him even better, you might want to read some of the other poems in *Leaves of Grass*.

Lisa Tracy
Walt Whitman Association
Camden, New Jersey

I hear America singing,

the varied carols I hear,

Those of mechanics, each one singing his as it should be blithe and strong,

The carpenter singing his as he measures his plank or beam,

The mason singing his as he makes ready for work, or leaves off work,

The boatman singing what belongs to him in his boat,

the deckhand singing on the steamboat deck,

The shoemaker singing as he sits on his bench,

the hatter singing as he stands,

The wood-cutter's song, the ploughboy's on his way in the morning,
or at noon intermission or at sundown,

The delicious singing of the mother, or of
the young wife at work,

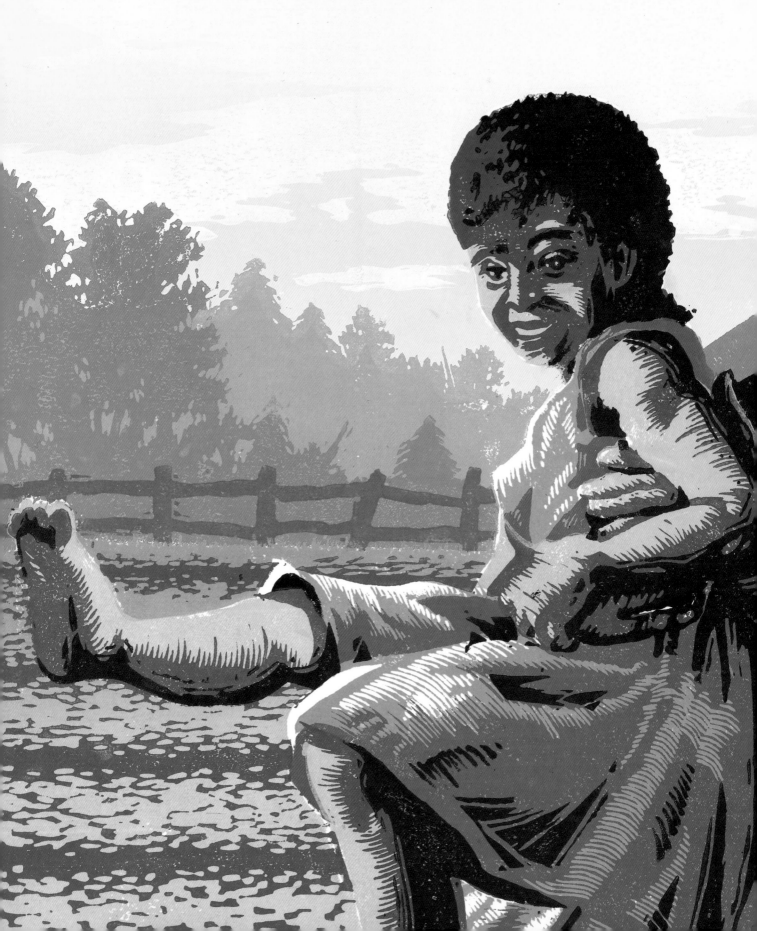

or of the girl sewing or washing,

Each singing what belongs to him or her and to none else,

The day what belongs to the day—at night the party of
    young fellows, robust, friendly,
Singing with open mouths their strong melodious songs.

I HEAR AMERICA SINGING

I hear America singing, the varied carols I hear,
Those of mechanics, each one singing his as it should be
  blithe and strong,
The carpenter singing his as he measures his plank or beam,
The mason singing his as he makes ready for work, or leaves off work,
The boatman singing what belongs to him in his boat, the deckhand
  singing on the steamboat deck,
The shoemaker singing as he sits on his bench, the hatter singing
  as he stands,
The wood-cutter's song, the ploughboy's on his way in the morning,
  or at noon intermission or at sundown,
The delicious singing of the mother, or of the young wife at work,
  or of the girl sewing or washing,
Each singing what belongs to him or her and to none else,
The day what belongs to the day—at night the party of young
  fellows, robust, friendly,
Singing with open mouths their strong melodious songs.

                                             —*Walt Whitman*